P9-CRA-753

THE RELEASE OF A LIVE PERFORMANCE

Sherry Kramer

BROADWAY PLAY PUBLISHING INC
224 E 62nd St, NY, NY 10065
www.broadwayplaypub.com
info@broadwayplaypub.com

First printing: December 2010
I S B N: 978-0-88145-447-5

Book design: Marie Donovan
Typographic controls: Adobe InDesign
Typeface: Palatino
Printed and bound in the U S A

CHARACTERS & SETTING

NELL, *late 20s, early 30s. Attractive.*

COCO, NELL's *older sister. Married, the mother of two. Husband doing quite well, financially. Hasn't been back home in years.*

BRENT, *early 30s. Always on the road. Drives cars to various locations on commission. No education. Loves to pick up hitchhikers and remembers everything they tell him, forever.*

SCOTT, BRENT's *latest hitchhiker. COCO's age. Wearing new Cowboy duds, which are the worse for wear. Went back to school and got his M B A last week. Getting married tomorrow—going into the wife's father's business. Taking a last look before he leaves single life all behind.*

Texas. The house NELL and COCO grew up in. Located just on the edge of the McClellan's Steak House parking lot, beneath the shadow of the huge plastic red and yellow cow, known as the FIST OF MEAT.

Necessary set pieces: a couch, a couple chairs, an antique table painted in pastel tones for a child's room, a small lamp in the window.

Basic layout of set: a bathroom off to stage right, the front door stage left, a window next to the door which looks out onto the parking lot.

August. A Tuesday night.

I suppose everybody finds, in a mistaken notion about another person, his one reason for living.

Yukio Mishima, *Forbidden Colors*

ACT ONE

(An ordinary living room, in a wooden frame house in a small town in Texas. The living room is decorated in the modest, but tasteful style of the middle class, circa 1960s. Some of the furniture suggests elegance—some of it is actually antique. A bit of lace and bric-a-brac indicates that the room was decorated by somebody's mother.)

(The room is filled with boxes and crates. Most of the boxes have various food logos on them—some are stamped SHIP TO McCLELLAN'S. There is a large Goodwill box, which COCO *makes sure gets its share.)*

*(*NELL *is standing at the window, looking out.)*

*(*COCO *has been doing all the packing, and continues.)*

*(*COCO *moves toward the door, holding a little antique table.* NELL *sees her, blocks her path.)*

NELL: Sometime bitch.

COCO: Don't start that with me—

NELL: *(Pulls the table away from* COCO*)* Little sometime bitch.

COCO: All right, then, talk to me. Tell me what you want to take, what you want to leave.

*(*NELL *takes the table over to the window.)*

COCO: Get away from that window. You hear me, Nell, you come away from that goddamn window and talk to me. You have been nailed to that goddamn window—

NELL: I like to see what's coming up the drive. Makes me feel like Scarlet O'Hara. You know what I'd say if I were Scarlet O'Hara?

COCO: No.

NELL: I'd say "Tomorrow is another lay."

COCO: What am I supposed to do when you say things like that? I don't know whether to laugh or cry.

NELL: You're lying to me and you're lying to yourself. If you'd admit it, you'd be a self-confessed liar. Now wouldn't that be something?

COCO: You called, and I came.

NELL: I called, you came, and you're moving furniture.

COCO: I told you I wanted to get started, moving things out to the car.

NELL: You did not.

COCO: I did so.

NELL: I didn't hear you.

COCO: Cause you were standing at that goddamn window looking at that damn ugly parking lot, thinking about him.

NELL: I'm not looking at the parking lot.

(COCO *comes over to the window, looks out. Swats at a mosquito)*

COCO: Damn it.

NELL: You missed it. Here. Let me.

(NELL *slaps* COCO's *back.)*

COCO: Get it?

NELL: Stand still.

(NELL *slaps again. Then again, harder. Chases* COCO
around the room, slapping)

COCO: Nell—

NELL: Stand still! *(She grabs* COCO, *pulls down her collar,
and looks at her neck.)* Jesusus, will you look at this!

COCO: Nell, what's wrong!

NELL: A nape...of...the...neck. HE'S GOT A NAPE OF
THE NECK TOO!

COCO: Let go of me, you hear!

NELL: Lord, Lord, he's got a nape of the neck—

(COCO *pushes* NELL *away, sending her sprawling into a
chair.)*

NELL: —and a chair! Damn if he doesn't have a chair
too! *(She climbs over the chair, stroking it.)* Jesusus, what
a miracle! Swing low, sweet chair-i-o-t. *(She tumbles
onto the floor.)* And he's got a floor. Got a rug too, I'll
bet. *(Runs her fingers through the rug)* Got a hundred
thousand closely threaded machine loomed fibers. I
think about them. I think about him. *(She crawls around
on the floor.)* He's got couch legs. Table bases. *(She is
at the door.)* Doors. Windows. *(Stands and looks outside
the window)* Drives. Outside of his house he's got—
(Pause) —an outside. *(She goes to one of the boxes, pulls
out a shirt.)* He's got a shirt. He's got all kinds of them.
He puts them on. He takes them off. Sometimes I see
shirts, and I want to see hundreds of 'em. I want to
see them around me, in front of me, behind me, back
through all recorded time. At times like that, I can't
help myself. I jump in the car and drive to Neiman
Marcus—the Men's Department.

   I run inside and I want to scream SHIRTS! ALL
THESE SHIRTS COULD BE HIS SHIRTS! He could
wear every shirt in the store. Oh Lord should you see
me in Neiman Marcus. I've almost died there. Twice

I've almost just pulled down a display on top of me and died.

The fucking wonder of it all, Coco—that's what I'm talking about! It's the miracle of shirts! Like the famous shroud of Turin. I see him there. In every one of them.

COCO: You hate Neiman Marcus.

NELL: That was before. Now I walk into Neiman Marcus—and they can't tell. I look like a perfectly normal person—no one can tell! And boy do I love walking down the street, mingling with all those damn normal people—riding the same buses, sitting at the same luncheonettes, eating the same tasteless food. How I'd love it, someday at the luncheonette, some one day when everybody is eating the same runny mashed potatoes, the same dry turkey slice, how I'd love to stand up some one day and scream "You poor slobs! You poor, ordinary himless slobs! You're eating this shit but I'm thinking of him!"

It's just one of those things. I just happen to love runny mashed potatoes and dry turkey slice. Always have.

COCO: Don't be angry with me. Don't say I can't say it's got to stop.

NELL: What about the luncheonettes? How will I stand the luncheonettes?

COCO: So you won't go.

NELL: Neiman Marcus?

COCO: Deep down inside you still hate Neiman Marcus.

NELL: What about the buses?

COCO: You have a car. You won't need, anymore, to take the bus.

NELL: Fact?

COCO: Fact.

NELL: You make these definite statements and I don't know who you are. I don't know how you know all these things you say you know. Tell me. How do you know them?

COCO: If on the bus, people remind you of him—if what you want is to stop—it's just common sense, Nell. It's just common sense to use your car.

NELL: He has a car, you know. If I get into my car, sit behind the wheel—

COCO: So walk.

NELL: You always were after my car.

COCO: Where do you get these ideas?

NELL: In the aftermath of a miracle there are no ideas. *(Pause)* Hold me, Coco.

COCO: No.

NELL: No? You said no to me? No sounds like a cold, hard fact.

COCO: Why should I hold you? It doesn't change anything, my holding you. If you want me to hold you so the world will go away, it's still there. If you're convinced it's actually, finally gone away, my holding you doesn't bring it back.
    Why should I hold you?

NELL: Good point.

COCO: *(She puts her arms out to NELL and holds her.)* Stop thinking about him.

NELL: You always were after my car, admit it.

COCO: Always.

NELL: Tell you what. I'll put it in writing. I'll leave you my car. I'll leave you my chair. I'll leave you my shirts.

COCO: *(Shaking her)* What are you talking about?

NELL: The one sure way to stop.

COCO: Little sometime bitch. You'd never have the guts.

NELL: Guts? The guts get thrown out with the bath water. With the car and the chair and the shirts.
  If I stop, will you take care of me? I'm pretty sure that once a person's separated from their guts, it's hard holding down a job.
  Will you take care of me?

COCO: I'm taking care of you now. If you'd let me.

NELL: It's too cold up where you live.

COCO: You get used to it.

NELL: Twenty years it takes to get used to it, that's how long it takes. I'll be an old woman by the time I get used to the cold. I'll be ready to move back down here.

COCO: The change'll do you good, Nell.

NELL: What will it change? I'll just be someplace cold, thinking about him.

COCO: So stop.

NELL: Just stop— *(Snaps her fingers)* —like that.
  It doesn't stop like that.
  Let me show you how it stops. *(Pause)* You see this chair? An ordinary chair.

COCO: Not the old chair trick.

NELL: It's a new trick.

COCO: It's still the old chair

NELL: No it isn't—that's the trick. Anyway, you love all my chair tricks.

COCO: You make these definite statements and—

NELL: You always have and you always will—

COCO: I never did. They're ordinary tricks.

NELL: You think turning a chair, a shirt, Neiman Marcus, and a luncheonette into him are ordinary tricks?

COCO: Yes.

NELL: Well, maybe.
  But here's the trick: To think about them, without thinking about him.
  You can't imagine what it's like when I try that trick.

COCO: I'm with you. I'll help you.

NELL: When I stop thinking about him there's nothing left. I'm all alone, and it's so hot—like the center of the earth—

COCO: Jesusus, not that center of the earth crap again. Don't you dare start in on the center of the earth. Don't you dare. You're right here. Here with me.

NELL: No, Coco. *You're* right here. Here with *me.*

COCO: It's just a story, that's all it is, Nell. The center of the earth is just a lovely, lovely story—

NELL: Is that what you think it is, Coco?

COCO: It's what you told me, Nell. It's what I have always believed.

NELL: That it was a story?

COCO: That it was lovely.

NELL: Here's what I didn't tell you: There's no way back.
    There isn't anything I can do that doesn't make me think of him and when I think of him there's nothing left worth doing. Nothing. For awhile I thought I had it licked. I took care of myself. I did things right. I felt the pleasure of doing things right. Things got very right for awhile around here—the house was very clean and

there was a lot of gourmet eating going on and I was to work on time and my bank balance was a piece of anal retentive art. Things got very right and I felt the pleasure of it, felt it fully, one day, for about thirty seconds.

That was my mistake. My first, last, and always mistake. My always.

I can make this chair—if I try very hard—I can make this ordinary chair *not* remind me of him. It's an act of the magic of hard work, but I'm not afraid of hard work. It can be done and I can do it. I can hard work systematically across this room like a mine sweeper, disengaging every snap, crackle and pop.

But I can't break the hold in here.

You walked into this house. You know—you must know—how warm and good it feels to have you walk into this house.

And everything it feels like is him.

COCO: Don't say things like that, Nell—

NELL: I called and you came but you can't change the trick. If I stop thinking about him I'll disappear.

COCO: You think you're so special. Oh, there was a time, there was a boy, and I thought like that. I have a story just like yours. Every woman has a story like that.

NELL: Some fact. Not my fact.

COCO: You remember him—no, you were too young, but he lived right down the street from us, in that big white house— *(She goes to the window, points.)* —right next to the— *(She can't find it.)* —well, it's gone now, but—

NELL: Everybody has the same story and everybody always tells it. Everybody has a story of a man they loved who didn't love them.

Everybody tells the story, then stands up at the end and says "But I'm here, aren't I? I didn't let it destroy

me, now did I?" And I don't know what to say.
  I don't know that for a fact.

COCO: It was an entertaining story. And it might have helped.

NELL: They never help.

COCO: It still might have.

NELL: Too late for entertaining stories.

COCO: It's too soon to get you packed, it's too late to tell you stories. Just what the hell did you call me down here for? Just what do you want me to do?

NELL: I want you to—hold me.

(COCO holds NELL tightly.)

NELL: You're a good hugger. You hug like mom.

COCO: You hug like mom.

NELL: Here comes an Uncle Paul hug—

(NELL tickles COCO, rubs and hugs her.)

COCO: Stop it—don't tickle me, Uncle Paul—please stop—

COCO/NELL: NOT UNTIL YOU STOP SAYING UNCLE! *(They hold each other for another few seconds.)*

COCO: *(Pulls away from NELL and slaps her.)* Damn you. This time bitch.

NELL: You feel it, don't you? Now you know it's real.

COCO: What's real about holding me and thinking about him? What's real about thinking about a man who never thinks about you? What? Nothing.

NELL: It's real.

COCO: Holding me and thinking about him—you've got your nerve.

NELL: Not you. I was holding Uncle Paul. He wouldn't mind. He'd understand. Uncle Paul, wherever you are—guess who loves you now. This time bitch loves you. Loves you so much, whenever she thinks about you she has to stop thinking about you and start thinking about him.

COCO: For God's sake, Nell. Stop.

NELL: The only way to stop is to spend time with people I hate. To have only very second rate times. Go to movies I don't like. Wear the kind of clothes I never wear. Now is that your idea of a way of life?

COCO: When we were kids we used to plan to live together. We used to plan to have so much fun.

NELL: You got your own kids now.

(The phone rings.)

COCO: Well? Aren't you going to answer it?

NELL: No. I always let the first one of the evening just ring right off the hook. Can't be too easy, right?

COCO: But—but it might be Steven— *(She moves toward the phone.)*

NELL: I said no. You let it ring.

COCO: But it might be Steven—something might have happened to one of the kids—

NELL: Jesusus, you called them the minute you got off the plane.

(COCO is about to pick up the phone.)

NELL: I'm warning you, Coco—

COCO: Don't be ridiculous, Nell— *(Starts to pick it up)*

NELL: I said NO!

(NELL pushes COCO away from the phone. COCO falls against some boxes.)

NELL: What's the matter with you? You can't be away from them for one day without— *(Pause)* You think about them a lot, don't you? About Steven, about the kids?

(The phone stops ringing.)

COCO: If that was Steven—

NELL: You think about them all the time, don't you?

COCO: What are you talking about? They're my life. My children.

NELL: All the time?

COCO: Yes. Yes, of course I do. It's a natural thing.

NELL: I'm sure it is.

COCO: They're my *children.*

NELL: You couldn't stop thinking about them, could you?

COCO: You don't understand.

NELL: Then what about Steven?

COCO: What about Steven?

NELL: Could you stop thinking about him? Not for long. For a minute. For two. Could you?

COCO: I wouldn't. Even if I could.

NELL: Then you could.

COCO: I didn't say that.

NELL: I'll make you a deal. You stop thinking about Steven—and I'll stop thinking about him. *(Pause)* Deal?

COCO: What kind of a deal is that?

NELL: An impossible deal. The kind of deal I like. Is it a deal? *(Pause)* I stop thinking about him. If you do. *(Pause)* We get in my car. I go with you, home. *(Pause)* Deal?

(NELL *extends her hand.* COCO *takes it.* NELL *is surprised.*)

COCO: Deal.

NELL: Deal. But don't try fooling me—cause I'll know.

COCO: How will you know?

NELL: About this. I'll know. Fact. *(She walks over to the phone.)* And here is what I also know. *(She holds her hand over the phone.)* There's someone picking up his phone. There's—anyone starting to dial my number. He reminds me totally of him. Watch carefully—this was the hardest part to learn how to do.

As far as I know, it's impossible to undo it.

(The phone rings.)

COCO: Don't answer it.

NELL: I always answer the second call. I just need to know, in my heart of hearts, that I haven't been too easy. Think mama would be proud? *(She puts her hand on the receiver, then pulls it back, teasing* COCO.*)* I'm going to pick up this phone and say hello. Hello is just a word, right? But you lop off the o, you've got hell. Uncouple the l's, you've got he. Take away the he, you got no one to say hello to. *(She picks up the phone.)* Hello? *(Laughs)* How are you?

COCO: Who is it? *(She runs over to the phone.)* Is it him?

NELL: *(To* COCO*)* Listen carefully, and tell me. *(To phone)* No, I can't. My sister's here visiting. I'm sorry the yes to no ratio isn't higher. *(Warm, generous laughter)*

COCO: Is it him? Nell, tell me, what's he want—what's he saying—

NELL: *(Waving at* COCO *to be quiet)* What—I can't— hello—hello— *(She holds the phone away from her.)* I didn't get to say good-bye.

COCO: Was it him, Nell—

NELL: Let's see what we can do with good-bye. Take off the *by* you've got good. Erase one *o* you've got God. Insert the deleted *o* in the discarded *by* you've got boy. Make a mistake with either one of those and you've got shit. *(She hangs up.)* You've got nothing.

COCO: Was it him!

NELL: Well—it was. But not the way you mean him.

COCO: Oh.

NELL: Maybe I should have let you talk to him.

COCO: Me? Why would I want to talk to him?

NELL: You wanted to know what he said.

COCO: That was only when I thought it was him.

NELL: *(Pause. Slyly)* It might be him next time, Coco. Would you like to talk to him then?

COCO: If it's him.

NELL: You would?

COCO: Yes.

NELL: Would you like to do more than talk to him?

COCO: What do you mean?

NELL: You're right. It's a stupid idea.

COCO: You wouldn't—would you? You wouldn't have him come over with me here? No, you wouldn't.

NELL: I just thought if you wanted to talk to him, you might as well have a good look at him, too. But it's a stupid—

COCO: No. I would. Like to.

NELL: You would?

COCO: Yes.

NELL: Deal.

COCO: But only—only if it's him.

NELL: That'll be up to you to decide.

COCO: What—

NELL: After all, to me they're all of them him.

(The phone rings.)

COCO: Just how am I supposed to know which—

NELL: You'll have to watch carefully. You'll have to catch the slight of man. Remember—the heart is quicker than the eye. *(She puts her hand on the receiver, then pulls back, teasing COCO again.)* I'll let you in on a little secret. The one that just called—that wasn't really him. Not really. *(Whispering)* But this is. *(She picks up the phone.)* Hello? Yes. Good to hear your voice. *(Aside to COCO)* Listen to the sound of my voice and tell me— is it him? *(To phone)* Yes, yes, no I love the heat. I was born to it. Born in it, took to it, can't live without it. Did you know it takes a person twenty years to adjust to a colder climate? Warmer one takes only three weeks. I read that somewhere. Well, I'd be dead by then. Yes. Cold did my sister in. At times. *(To COCO)* Well? What do you think you're willing to risk? *(To phone)* Hang on, just one second. *(To COCO)* Take a chance. What can you lose?

COCO: What if I say yes? Say it's him?

NELL: You get to talk to him.

COCO: But what if it isn't really him?

NELL: Oh, you can talk to as many as you like—as long as you think that it's him.

COCO: All right. *(She reaches for the phone.)*

NELL: You do?

COCO: Yes.

NELL: Good. *(She hands COCO the phone.)* It's your husband.

COCO: Steven—I—no, we're not driving back till morning. I told you we might not. Oh. It's in the top drawer. You called me because—it's always there. *(She laughs softly.)* I love you. *(She hangs up.)*

NELL: You didn't ask him over. And here I thought we had us a deal.

COCO: Steven wants you with us too. And the kids— Jeffery adores you.

NELL: You're not listening to me. We had a deal.

COCO: You're talking to hear yourself talk.

NELL: Fact?

COCO: I love you. Doesn't that make a difference?

NELL: It makes all the difference. And it doesn't change a thing.

COCO: What would it change? Answer me—what would it change?

NELL: It doesn't change this— *(She goes to the phone, picks up the receiver, and puts it to her head.)* Click. Russian Roulette.

COCO: You're breaking my heart.

NELL: Your heart? You're not here because I'm breaking your heart. You're here because I'm breaking mine. *(Putting the receiver back)* What will you do when he gets here?

COCO: Wait for him to leave.

NELL: I thought you wanted to talk to him. Look at him. Get up close and feel the heat.

COCO: It's too damn hot already. And that smell. It never used to smell like that.

NELL: That's the smell of the seventy-two ounce steak, over at McClellan's.

COCO: How do you stand it?

NELL: You get used to it. Look. You can see it from here.

(NELL *takes* COCO *over to the window*)

NELL: See? Capital M little c Big C-L-E double L-A-N-S. McCLELLAN'S. You can see the underside of the polyvinyl cow.

COCO: I think it's making me sick.

NELL: Aw, come on, Coco. Right at this very minute, there's men over there, eating it. The seventy-two ounce steak. I mean, think about it. A seventy-two ounce—

COCO: I'm gonna be sick—

NELL: Come on then—

(NELL *leads* COCO *over to the couch.*)

COCO: Don't, Nell—

NELL: But you're sick—

(NELL *makes her lie down with her head in her lap.*)

COCO: Don't, Nell—stop it—

NELL: Just put your little head down—

COCO: *(Trying to get up)* I said don't baby me, Nell—

NELL: Stay where you are. Any minute now, that phone's gonna ring. Wouldn't it be nice, just to stay like this until it rings?

COCO: Maybe it won't ring.

NELL: And you, come all the live long day to hear it ring. To watch him walk into this room. If it didn't ring, what would you do?

COCO: Stay like this.

NELL: You're lying to me, and you're lying to yourself. If you'd admit it you'd be a—

COCO: Why do we think that line is so funny?

COCO/NELL: A SELF-CONFESSED LIAR.

NELL: It will ring.

COCO: You still don't have to answer it.

NELL: Here are some truths: Dust to dust. Birth death taxes. One plus one equals the phone will ring and I will answer.

COCO: Remember what we used to say when mama said things like that? When she'd say things like "You *have* to be in by ten" or "That bed of yours *has* to be made?"

NELL: What'd we say?

COCO: We'd say "What about the bomb, mama? What if the bomb falls first? I won't have to make my bed, mama, if the bomb falls first."

NELL: The bomb ain't falling before that phone rings, Coco.

COCO: Fact?

NELL: Fact. If the bomb were dropping in, it would call first. This is what it would be like: Ding, dong. A-bomb falling.

COCO: *(Laughing)* You are the sometime terrible. The sometime worst. *(Pause)* Nell? Tell me a story.

NELL: What kind of story.

COCO: Any kind of lovely, lovely story.

NELL: Bed time story?

COCO: I already know the one about the three little pigs.

NELL: BED time story. Story about time in bed.

COCO: Oh, God. I don't know if I'm ready for this.

NELL: Jerry the Sailor. A True Bed Time Story.

COCO: Oh, God. Not a sailor.

NELL: And just what do you think you know about sailors?

COCO: Everybody knows about sailors.

NELL: You do not. You know one line about all sailors— "a girl in every port and any port in a storm." That's all you know, right?

COCO: All right—right. Fact.

NELL: Fact. You're right. So lie back, and relax. *(She places* COCO's *head in her lap again.)* The True Story of Jerry the Sailor. You'll like it. It's a lovely, lovely story.
    Jerry the Sailor was a scuba diver who lived by the sea. I lay down with Jerry the Sailor because he bandaged my knee.

COCO: Is it over yet?

NELL: On the night I met Jerry the Sailor, he was on his way South to the sea.
    I lay down with Jerry the Sailor because of the way he—bandaged my knee.

COCO: Jesusus, not a refrain.

NELL: Buck up, will you? The one who's calling any minute now, most likely I lay down with him for reasons that will never rhyme with anything.

COCO: Okay, okay, get it over with.

NELL: Coco! That's no way to listen to a lovely, lovely story!

COCO: What's so lovely about it?

NELL: It's a story about him, Coco. All the stories about him are lovely.
    In this story, this is what he said when he met me.

He said: "You look like the kind of girl who could
get some depth." Depth is the thing scuba divers talk
about wanting. So how can it help but be a lovely
story—it's about him when he knew how to use a
huge, cold ocean, and a thin rubber skin to stay warm.

It's about him when he was the man who when
we finally fell asleep that night turned to me, and
said, so sweetly: "Pleasant dreams. I'll nail you in the
morning."

COCO: Oh, God.

NELL: I'll nail you in the morning. It's what they
must have said to Jesus Christ. I looked it up. "*Clavis
confligero te mane.*"

COCO: What?

NELL: That's Latin for "I'll nail you in the morning."

COCO: I'm cold. So cold.

(NELL *wraps* COCO *up in her arms, and continues, sweetly.*)

NELL: On the night I met Jerry the Sailor, he forgot
all about that Sea. Listen: This is the story of how he
bandaged my knee.

He smiled at me. He smiled at me and he held up the
mercurochrome and he dipped in the swab. It came out
that wild, popsickle orange and I asked him, "Does it
hurt?"

He smiled at me. He smiled at me and he said, so
sweetly, he said "No. It doesn't hurt."

He smiled at me as he ran the swab along the cut and
it hurt like hell.

I asked him again. "Does it hurt?" He held the swab
to the deepest part of the cut, and he said, so sadly,
"Don't you trust me?" he said.

He said it again: "It doesn't hurt." He smiled at me as
he said it again and I lay down with him.

Now isn't that a lovely, lovely story?

COCO: What do you want from me, Nell? When you tell me a story like that I don't know whether to laugh or cry.

NELL: You're lying to me and you're—

COCO: STOP IT! I *DON'T* KNOW!

NELL: Coco, I can't believe that. You always know.

COCO: Why do you want me to say it's a lovely story when you know I can't?

NELL: I don't know that.

COCO: It's not a lovely, lovely story. Not to me. Not to ME!

(COCO *tries to get away from* NELL. NELL *holds her back.*)

NELL: (*Snaps her fingers*) I know why you don't like it. I forgot to tell you the happy ending. I forgot to tell you what Jerry the Sailor said to me in the end.

COCO: Did you ever see him again?

NELL: Course I didn't.

COCO: Then who cares what he said.

NELL: He said some very interesting things. For a sailor.

COCO: It doesn't matter what he said.

NELL: Watch it. You're beginning to slip.

COCO: Fact. It doesn't matter to me what he said. Fact.

NELL: Two wrongs don't make a right. But three rights make a left. You figure it out.

COCO: He was a goddamn nobody, a nothing, a scum, and you let him—

NELL: Take that back. You take that back!

COCO: They are all of them nothing. What's happened to you?

NELL: You know the rules. You take it back.

COCO: All right. All right. But it's still a fact. He's gone.

NELL: A nothing can't be gone.

COCO: I said I was sorry.

NELL: *(Pause)* I was telling you what Jerry the Sailor said.

COCO: I'll nail you in the morning is what that goddamn—

NELL: Try it in Latin. It's even sweeter in the Latin. But it's so—so absolute in the original. So—so choiceless.
    I think you'd better say it in Latin. Go on, I'll help you. Say it.

COCO: No.

NELL: No?

COCO: No.

NELL: *(Pause)* Then I guess I'll have to finish my story. I guess I'll have to tell you what Jerry the Sailor said.
    He said I was tight. Like a hooker. And he asked me, did I do those exercises hookers do. *(Pause)*

Come on, Coco. Ask me about those exercises. I can't finish the story unless you express some interest in the exercises. *(No response)* Ask me about those exercises, Coco, or this story will go on and on.

COCO: *(Barely audible)* Tell me about those exercises.

NELL: What?

COCO: Tell me about those exercises.
    The exercises hookers do.

NELL: Now 'a days, everybody does 'em. They say that the woman who does them daily, religiously, has got the benefit of a very soft, very deep, very warm hand.

COCO: Who the hell wants a hand there?

NELL: My sentiments exactly. I don't know one man who wouldn't scream like a son of a bitch if he climbed in and found a hand in there. Still, the body of literature about its effect on men—mostly found in women's magazines—the body of literature, to sum it up, says: Show me the penis stroked and held and fondled far inside the well-trained vagina, and I'll show you a happy penis. *(Pause)* Of course, you couldn't really show it.

But there's another reason for doing the exercises. *(Whispers)* They make you have a new orgasm.

COCO: What's wrong with the one I have?

NELL: This one's all improved. They even have a name for it—like a Z-sports car, or brand X. They call it—the G Orgasm.

COCO: You didn't try it, did you?

NELL: It's not as if I needed one...but then I thought, don't be afraid of progress. You know how I'm always saying "the future is here"? I thought, maybe it's a little lower. *(Pause)* But I didn't have it. The exercises don't do you any good, you do them once.

COCO: What good do they do you if you do them more?

NELL: They make you come like a man.

COCO: Bullshit.

NELL: Scientific fact.

COCO: Scientific bullshit.

NELL: You never wanted to come like a man?

COCO: No.

NELL: Me neither. So what we have here is a double golden opportunity of becoming self-confessed liars.

COCO: Fact?

COCO/NELL: Fact.

COCO: A woman can't come like a man. Not even in a story.

NELL: You wouldn't like to try to just once? I can show you the exercise. Come on, Coco. Just once?

(COCO shrugs.)

NELL: Lie down. On your back.

(COCO lies down on her back.)

NELL: Now. They say to start with a swimming pool. I want you to understand that somebody else, they'd start you off with a swimming pool. Not me. I mean, sure, it's clear and blue, but it's not real water, you know? It's used water. And besides, the neighbor's kids have been pissing in it. That's why I prefer the Aegean Sea.

Ready? Here we go. *(Softly)* Imagine that you are lying on the fine, white sand on the shore of the Aegean Sea. It is a clear...warm...bright summer day.

COCO: Why the Aegean Sea?

NELL: The Aegean's a sea you can see all in one place. It doesn't move around a lot like the big seven do. And it's warm. All that land around it makes it warm. Imagine doing it with the Arctic Ocean—you're talking icebergs, you're talking chunks of dirty gray ice the size of Manhattan.

The Aegean Sea is more green than blue, they say— I've never seen it. I suppose there are more things in a sea than there are in swimming pools—tuna and sharks and lots of microscopic swimming things—but I just can't picture doing it with a concrete, chlorinated pool. What would be the point?

Are you relaxed now?

That little talk was supposed to relax you. Get you primed.

Imagine you are lying on your back on the fine, hard white sand on the shore of the Aegean Sea. You are looking up at the sky. It is more blue than any blue you have ever seen.

You part your legs slightly.

(COCO *does*.)

NELL: They open onto the bright, clear water. You hear the sound of the waves, breaking gently.

You close your eyes. You draw in, with something inside you. It takes a moment or two, but gradually the water begins flowing up between your legs. The movement of the water feels—it feels—full. Whatever it is between your legs can suck, can pull, you suck and pull with. The water rushes in, past every soft, smooth place inside you.

By now you know for sure where it is inside you that can suck and pull. By now you know how good it feels. By now you are ready to stop. Already ten's of thousands of gallons have emptied into you. The level of the Aegean Sea, if you looked—but you don't look, you keep your eyes closed, you keep on sucking in—by now the level of the water is two, then five, then twenty feet lower, if you looked you'd see the great Aegean Sea shrinking, you'd see it funneling, disappearing into you, and you'd stop. But you don't stop. You'd see the slime and rock exposed banks, the naked bottom of the sea, the countless water creatures, gasping in the air, and you'd stop. You can't stop. You keep on, sucking in and in.

And it feels wonderful, and it feels full and it will never fill you. Never.

(*The phone rings.* NELL *starts for it eagerly, then hesitates. She looks over to* COCO, *then goes to the phone and picks up the receiver. She holds the receiver like a gun to her head for an instant.*)

NELL: Pow. *(Pause)* Hello? *(Pause)* No. You don't have
to tell me who this is. I know who this is.
   I guess I knew it would be you.
   Brent—you didn't. Not the seventy-two ounce steak.
Oh, no, Brent, you didn't—you did. The seventy-two
ounce steak—no, oh no, you're not coming over here.
You'll be sick, you'll be sick all over the—no, I didn't
mean that. No, I want you to. Please, come over.
   Please. *(She hangs up.)* That was Brent. Calling from
beneath the huge fist of meat. Calling from McClellan's
to say "A-bomb falling."
   He's a sometimes sweet man. He'll be sick all over
the floor. *(She goes to the bathroom, puts the toilet seat up
and hangs the bath mat out of the way.)* Well, Coco, I guess
the gun was loaded. Coco— *(She walks over to* COCO.*)*
Coco, you asleep? *(She prods* COCO *with her foot.)* Coco,
you all right?

COCO: *(Sits up. Angry)* I almost had it.

NELL: Had what?

COCO: The Aegean Sea.

NELL: Don't be ridiculous.

COCO: I almost had it all inside me.

NELL: Almost is never a fact.

*(*COCO *lies back down, closes her eyes.)*

NELL: Coco—what are you doing?

COCO: Leave me alone.

NELL: Didn't you hear me, Coco? He's coming. Brent's
coming. *(Pause. No response)* I guess you knew that.
   But here's what you didn't know. *(Leans down,
whispers in her ear)* He's picked up a hitchhiker, and
he's bringing him along. For you. *(Stands up)* He's
coming, Coco. And he's bringing somebody for you.
(The phone rings.)

NELL: Why don't you get that, Coco. It might be Steven, you know. *(No response)* Coco? COCO!

(The phone continues to ring. When it stops, NELL takes it off the hook.)

NELL: This time, Coco. This time—him. *(She goes to her window, and waits.)*

(Blackout)

END OF ACT ONE

ACT TWO

(BRENT *and* SCOTT *come stumbling across the parking lot.
As they come up the front steps* NELL *opens the door.)*

(BRENT, *holding his hand over his mouth and gagging,
streaks through the room and makes it to the bathroom. He
closes the door behind him. The faint sounds of him getting
sick.)*

(SCOTT *is several instants behind him. He lurches into the
living room. He doesn't see* NELL, *who is behind the door.
He is very, very drunk.)*

SCOTT: *(To* COCO, *who is still lying on the floor)* Did he
make it?

(BRENT *makes a loud retching noise.)*

SCOTT: See, Brent, I tole you you'd make it. Tole the ole
boy he'd make it. And I'm gonna make it. *(Singing)*
I'm getting married in the morning
Ding, dong, the bells are gonna chimmmmmeee—
(Goes over to COCO, *squats down over her prone body
and speaks confidentially)* You ever notice the Freudian
implications of that song? They're there all right. You
start off—he's getting married in the morning. Now
what, you say, what is so fuckin' accordion Freudian
about that? Well, I'll tell you. It's like this. It's like from
the beginning of recorded time.
      You know the story of Abraham and Isaac?
Everybody knows the story of Abraham and Isaac.
Everybody knows God said "Take him out and cut him

open. Sacrifice him. To me."

Everybody knows how it turned out. What they don't know, is that God specifically specified for it to happen in the morning. God said "Abe, babe, you gotta slip out early in the morning, before Sarah wakes up and sees you on the lam." On the lamb— *(He "baaas" like a lamb.)* —get it? "Sneak out before the bitch throws a monkey wrench" is what he probably said. Cause God was wise to the ways of women. Think he would have gotten a tumble if he'd asked Sarah to go out and take a kitchen knife to the joy of her old age? No Way.

And so it has been, even unto this day. A man wants to go hunting, fishing, a man wants to do any of the things a man wants to do a woman doesn't want him to, he sneaks out to do it in the morning.

I don't mind telling you, I insisted on a morning wedding.

But it doesn't stop there. No sir.

I'm getting married in the morning

Ding dong de dumdum dumdum daaaaa"

Dong, get it? Oh yeah, ding dong the bells are gonna *chime*. That's what happens, all right. Ring 'em and they chime. Cause ole Brent's gonna get me to the church on time. *(He bends down and looks at* Coco *closely.)* You look familiar. But that don't mean anything. You all look alike. *(Looks at her some more)* Funny. From what Brent told me I figured you'd be taller. *(He takes off his cowboy hat with his left hand, a sweeping gesture over* Coco's *body.)* Allow me to introduce myself. I'm a buddy of ole Brent's—picked me up outside of Houston. See, I'm hitching my way to get hitched. I'm getting married in the morning, see, so I'm hitching my way to get—aw, forget it. *(He extends his right hand. It is severely deformed. All the fingers are fused into one, the skin stretched tightly over them.)*

I'm— *(His hand closes over* Coco's.*)*

COCO: SCOTT!

(COCO opens her eyes. SCOTT helps her up.)

SCOTT: Scott Kelley.

COCO: SCOTT KELLEY!

SCOTT: Scott Kelley.

COCO: SCOTT KELLEY!!! My God— *(She's up, animated, excited.)* —my God, I never would have recognized you from you face—it's you, Jesusus, it's Scott Kelley! Nell, it's SCOTT KELLEY!

SCOTT: Scott Kelley.

COCO: You grew up! I never thought of you growing up.

SCOTT: *(Defensive)* Why wouldn't I? Just what do you mean by that?

COCO: I just meant you'd changed.

SCOTT: Oh. Well, everybody does.

COCO: I suppose I have too.

SCOTT: What?

COCO: Changed.

SCOTT: Yeah, sure, sure you have. *(Tries to be more enthusiastic)* You sure have.

COCO: It's been—oh, Jesus, let me see—

SCOTT: Oh, five years at least.

COCO: Five? More like—fifteen. More like—

SCOTT: Oh, yeah. Fifteen, sure.

COCO: You don't remember me?

SCOTT: Well, I—

COCO: You don't remember me? But you have to remember me—you said I looked familiar, that's the first thing you said, "You look familiar".

SCOTT: So? You do. It doesn't mean anything. After awhile, you all—

NELL/SCOTT: —look alike.

SCOTT: Right. (*He cocks his head to one side and looks* NELL *over carefully, then continues.*) See, it's—it's not really fair. Everyone remembers me because of this— (*Indicates his hand*) I meet somebody, talk to them for ten seconds at a party, five years later they remember me, because of my hand. People always saying "Hello Scott" to me, in a hallway, on the street, I don't know them from Adam. It's not fair. People smiling at me at the grocery store. You got to understand. There's just one of me, and all of you. (*Pause*) I'm sorry.

COCO: But I'm Carol Crandal. Little Carol Crandal. You're the one who called me Coco. Coco Loco.

SCOTT: (*Shrugs*) Sorry.

COCO: But—but I was there when it happened. I was there. Staring up from the ground, watching you. I watched you fall. I ran for help. He was climbing this tree, Nell. The tree no one was supposed to climb, the high tension wires, they came up out of the ground, but Scott said any two year old could tell the difference between a wire and a branch—

SCOTT: (*Looking at both hands, as if comparing them*) "The difference between a wire and a branch."

COCO: —and I was standing there, watching him climb, watching—

SCOTT: You were there when I went down?

COCO: Right there.

SCOTT: Aren't many people left who remember me going down. I don't remember. Last thing I remember—well, I don't remember the last thing I remember. I remember that I should remember reaching out my hand. *(He reaches out.)* Next thing I knew was—see, I don't even know what the next thing I knew was. My doctor says I blocked. I was just a little kid, but he told me I blocked. So I get this picture in my head—this picture of this linebacker, all suited up, big guy, enormous guy, huge—and he's got the ball under one arm— *(He tucks his right hand under his arm, hiding it.)* —and the other's out like this— *(Left hand out, blocking)* —and he's running. He's running like a son of a bitch. And there's doctors coming at him with scalpels and swabs—WHAM. And there's my parents crying— *(Unsteady)* —wham. *(Builds to anger again)* And there's candy and toys and kids whose hands look like hands—WHAM! *(Softly)* And there's—there's this tree—this tree—God, it's big...it's...it's... *(Screaming)* WHAM! WHAM!! WHAM!!

I turn around and look behind me. It's all gone. There's nothing to remember. *(Pause)* I could say I remember you. I'd like to. I mean, think about it. You come all this way, out in the middle of no where, and you find yourself someone who was there.

COCO: But it was right here, Scott. Right here—

(COCO drags SCOTT over to the window.)

COCO: You lived right over—

SCOTT: What are you talking about?

COCO: You lived right over there!

SCOTT: Shit! Really?

COCO: Right over— *(She points again.)*

SCOTT: There? Nothing but a damn parking lot over there.

COCO: You lived right there.

SCOTT: Well. Goddamn. Goddamn! Really? Goddamn. *(He goes out on the porch, takes a good look.)*

Goddamn! Here I am, in the middle of nowhere, and I'm right there! *(He looks in the window at* COCO.*)* I have to say it—small world.

NELL: He has to say it—small world.

COCO: If it were such a fucking small world he'd remember me, now wouldn't he, Nell? It's not a small world.

NELL: Okay, okay—

COCO: It's huge!

SCOTT: *(Coming back inside)* It must have been quite a sight. It must have been something to see! Tell me—uh—Coco—what was it like?

COCO: You can go to hell.

SCOTT: Yeah? You're absolutely right. That's just exactly what it was like.

Like sitting in your living room, playing Monopoly, and picking up a card. An ordinary, harmless looking card. Turning it over and it says "Go To Hell. Do Not Pass Go. Do Not Collect No Two Hundred Dollars." *(Pause. To* NELL*)* We haven't been properly introduced.

NELL: We need to be?

SCOTT: You got to understand. Here I am, in the unusual position of not knowing Coco here all my life, while I feel like with you, it's just the opposite.

*(*COCO *is packing, making a great deal of noise, angry at* SCOTT*.)*

*(*SCOTT *extends his left hand.* NELL *puts out her right, then corrects, and puts out her left. He has switched and puts out his right. She puts out her right again.)*

SCOTT: I used to shake with my left because I can't feel a damn thing with my right.

(The switching continues throughout SCOTT's *speech, Groucho Marx style.)*

SCOTT: It bothered me. You're supposed to find out so much about another person's character from their handshake. Whether you can trust 'em. Whether they cheat on their wife. Whether they take the Lord's name in vain. You're supposed to find out all that—just from holding their hand. With this lump, what could I tell? Zip.

Then it dawned on me. Zip was exactly what they were finding out about me!

*(*SCOTT *grabs* NELL's *right hand with his right hand. She can't help looking at it. He pulls her to him and kisses her, making free with his left hand as well.)*

SCOTT: Works like a charm. Every time. *(Pause)* Well?

NELL: *(Still holding his hand)* Truthful. Faithful. God fearing.

SCOTT: Yeah. Well, but only after years in expensive therapy, squeezing raw eggs. *(Pause)* They charge by the egg. *(Pause)* I'm getting married in the morning.

NELL: So you said.

SCOTT: This is my final fling. My own private bachelor party. I had this idea, of cutting a swath across the Continent. Of drinking. Driving. Womanizing. Can you imagine what that's like?

NELL: Yes.

SCOTT: You can?

NELL: Yes.

SCOTT: I couldn't. That's why I had to do it.

NELL: Dancing on tables. Closing bars down. Driving across the border to another state. Doing it again.

SCOTT: Yeah.

NELL: Your arm across the shoulders of a man you've just met and who you'd swear you'd die for.

SCOTT: Yeah.

NELL: The two of you plow your way to the blind side of the local First National Trust. You face the wall, unzipping your pants. There it is. What a picture. Two men, their legs slightly spread, making a night deposit. "A night deposit" one of you says to the other. "We're making a night deposit."

SCOTT: Yeah. Yeah!

NELL: A woman beneath you making sounds it excites you to know you will never hear again.

SCOTT: *(Softly)* Yeah. *(Pause)* I wanted to feel like General Sherman, sweeping across Georgia. I wanted to use it all up, everything I could find. I wanted to turn around, and see it all smoking, all in flames behind me. I wanted to walk down that aisle, and when I looked back behind me—

NELL: Wham.

SCOTT: *(Whispers)* Wham. *(He moves to take NELL in his arms.)*

BRENT: *(The door to the bathroom swings open. He stumbles out.)* God, that was incredible. I feel awful. *(He makes it to the couch, reeling. Then he pulls himself together.)* I was driving—driving west, like I always do, driving west and looking for the sign. A sign like that, coming up on you out of the night like a reddish yellow harvest McClellan moon, it's hard not to follow it. I followed it like I always do, but something happened. I got lost. I got confused. I must have been following the wrong moon. That's when I decided that tonight would be the night.

You let them know, right when you walk in under the big cow, through the swinging doors, so they give

you the special table. It's the best table in the house.
You get your own waiter, too.

As soon as you sit down you have to sign this release.
I guess they've had guys croak on them, choking on a
piece of meat. They've got this real sharp knife hanging
on the wall behind the table, and the maitre d' knows
how to use it in an emergency, so you have to sign this
release saying if he botches it, if he tries to save you
and he botches it, you agree not to sue.

I guess their normal restaurant insurance covers them
if you strangle eating a normal dinner, on your own.

You got to eat the seventy-two ounce steak, the
tossed salad, the shrimp cocktail, the vegetable medley,
the twice baked potato, and the pie-a-la-mode, all in an
hour.

You eat it all in an hour, you don't have to pay.

You get it all down, they carve your name with a
branding iron on a big wooden plaque.

My name's on that plaque.

They show you the rules.

No talking to customers at other tables.

No eating on the floor.

No throwing up.

Your waiter accompanies you to the john and I mean
accompanies. They got a large stall built special. He
watches you like a hawk. Checks the toilet paper when
you blow your nose. You throw up even a little bit, you
got to pay.

You also got to pay, you want anything other than
coffee or tea, like a Coke or something.

They let you order it any way you want. They ask
you do you want it Rare. Medium Rare. Raw. Well. I
ordered it extra well. I mean, you go to McDonalds,
you get a quarter pounder, that's a quarter of a pound
before cooking, right, and what do you get, you get
nothing, right? So I figured, seventy-two ounces, that's
four and a half pounds, that'd be eighteen times

nothing.

The waiter made this funny face when he took my order.

I stepped outside for some fresh air. They let you go out side while it's cooking. Your hour doesn't start till the platter hits the table.

My waiter came out and gave me a five minute warning, just as a courtesy, he didn't have to. I sat down at my table. I made sure everything was as it should be. I tested the steak knife hanging on the wall behind me.

It was sharp all right. It was something like a surgeon would use.

It was much sharper than the knife next to my plate.

The platter hit the table. In that instant, I developed my strategy. I would cut the steak into fourths, and eat one fourth at the top of every quarter. I would finish out the rest of the time in the side dishes. The waiter, who was clocking me with a large stopwatch, and a true professional, I might add, graciously agreed to sound a small bell at appropriate intervals.

I picked up my fork and steak knife.

You talk about your fatal errors. You talk about your fatal flaws. Everybody has them.

Seventy-two ounces of shoe leather. Seventy-two ounces of gristle and fat and flesh, charred beyond recognition. Seventy-two ounces of open-hearthed petrified prime. I tossed my knife and fork over my shoulder. They were as good as useless to me now.

I was able to rip the thing in half. I had to stand up to do it—they let you stand up. I was reminded and inspired by a painting I once saw of Jacob wrestling with the angel. It was a lot like that.

My waiter watched me. I saw that funny look on his face again. "Wipe that grin off your face" I wanted to tell him. No, no. Save your strength, I reminded myself. Then it came to me.

That funny look—that funny look was pity.
I could understand the difficulty of his position. He
was working for the house. He couldn't, being the
professional he was, warn me, influence my ordering
decision. He'd put in the order for extra well, knowing
full well what it meant. Still, he treated me with
respect, and I respected him for that.
I started chewing on the larger half. I wanted to give
myself an edge.
My waiter sounded the first quarter. I'd barely made
it past the outer crust on the pointed end. I started to
panic. The waiter reached across and wiped my
forehead with the napkin he had draped over his arm.
I'd never actually seen a waiter use the napkin they've
always got over their arm, so I was doubly grateful.
I realized I needed a psychological boost here,
something to keep me going, give me hope. The
shrimp cocktail caught my eye. It was only four jumbo
gulf shrimp, drenched in a plentiful helping of sauce.
I reached for my fork—it's hard to break the habits of
a lifetime—then picked up the dish— *(He starts to act
out events.)* —it was in like a kind of sherbet cup—and
tossed it back. I could feel the shrimp gliding, coasting
down my throat. Once again, I nodded my head at my
waiter, thankfully. I felt sure that the extra sauce had
been his doing.
I took up the chunk of meat in my hands. I dove into
it, buried my face in it, determined to eat my way
through to the light. *(He is beginning to relive the story.
Puts his hands to his face and chews, getting out of breath)*
The bell rang. It had a far off sound, as if it were
coming from another world. I stayed where I was,
chewing, ripping, swallowing, submerged.
Again, the bell.
Fifteen minutes left. I stuffed the rest of the piece of
flesh down my throat. I gagged, kept on swallowing,
come on, come on, you can do it. My fists struck the

table. One. Two.

I was in trouble. I saw my waiter glancing nervously in the direction of the razor sharp steak knife. THREE. I got it down. I took a deep, beautiful breath.

"Close call" my waiter said. We both looked at the knife hanging on the wall behind me.

I jumped up. My hand snaked out, reaching the knife an instant before his did. I tore it off the wall.

Our eyes met.

"My decision" I said.

I was able to slash the remaining half of the steak into eight long slices before the knife gave out.

I ate one of them. Then two. Then three. *(His breathing becomes more labored.)* The tossed salad. That looks easy. Sure that will go down, all that dressing. Two handfuls, in, swallow, can't feel it going down, that feels good.

Two more pieces of meat, don't chew, no time to chew, just swallow, swallow. Damn you, swallow. Another. Swallow. Another. *(Panting. Looks around, disoriented)* The baked potato. Yes. *(Tries to jam it in his mouth)* Won't fit. WON'T FIT! Tear it in half.

Vegetable. Don't forget your vegetables.

Okay. Okay. What? What? *(Despair)* One minute? One? *(Hysteria)* ONE MINUTE! Apple pie—where's that bitch—that apple pie—Jesus Christ—

Thirty seconds? Two slices left—swallow, swallow— fifteen seconds—one piece left, one— *(He's choking, gagging.)* —get it in—GET IT IN! SWALLOW! Five seconds—five-four three-two-one-SWALLOW!!!!!

The bell! The bell! *(Exhausted)* The waiter slammed me up against the wall and pinned me while the maitre d' pried my mouth open and looked inside with a flashlight. But I was clean.

It was every bit of it gone.

They frisked me quickly, quietly, efficiently. They knew their business. Mac McClellan himself came over to congratulate me. My waiter hugged me and went off to heat up the branding iron.

They blew a whistle, so everybody stopped eating during the engraving ceremony, and when it was over, everybody cheered. *(He pushes his fist into the air, the victor, and stands there triumphant, in all his glory.)* Now I ask you. Have you ever heard a story like that before?

NELL: Two, three times a week.

BRENT: What?

NELL: I hear it all the time.

BRENT: Not like mine, you don't.

NELL: Exactly like yours.

BRENT: Maybe they start off like mine—maybe they start off sounding like mine at the start—but when I get to the moment when I reach for that knife—when I grab that knife and tear it off the wall—

NELL: They go through seven knives a week, Brent.

BRENT: What?

NELL: And I've lost track of the times they've had to replaster that wall.

BRENT: What are you talking about?

NELL: They all, Brent, every last one of 'em, order it extra well. *(Pause)* But did it make you happy?

BRENT: But my waiter, he acted like—when I went for the knife—he acted like it was the next closest thing to an act of God.

(SCOTT is standing inside the doorway.)

BRENT: Didn't he, Scott? Didn't he!

SCOTT: He did. It's a fact. He sure did.

BRENT: He was there. *(He grabs SCOTT and drags him over to NELL.)* He'll tell you. I was magnificent!

SCOTT: Ole Brent was magnificent.

NELL: You are all of you—

(BRENT *crumples to the floor.*)

NELL: —magnificent. But did it make you—

BRENT: All of a sudden, I don't feel so good.

SCOTT: *(To* NELL*)* Well. Where were we? I think we were somewhere.

(SCOTT *kisses* NELL. *She does not respond.*)

NELL: Brent—

(BRENT *moans.* NELL *shoves* SCOTT *away and goes to* BRENT.*)

NELL: You should go in there— *(Pointing to the bedroom)* —you should go lie down.

BRENT: In there? You're not getting me in there tonight.

NELL: You should lie down.

BRENT: I'm lying down. See? This is down, and I'm lying. If I moved, I think I'd die.

NELL: You'll feel better if I get you something hot to drink—

BRENT: NO ! Lord, no! *(He holds his hand over his mouth.)*

SCOTT: *(Comes up behind* NELL, *strokes her hair)* Hey, I remember where we were. It isn't very far from here. If we leave now, we can be there in no time—

COCO: Wait a minute, Scott—Nell, what about me?

NELL: *(Trying to get away from* SCOTT*)* Did it—Brent, listen to me—did it make you happy?

BRENT: Happy? What the hell are you talking about?

SCOTT: We'll take the express.

COCO: Scott—please.

BRENT: Do I look happy?

SCOTT: I've expressed a desire to take the express.

(SCOTT *drags* NELL *down on the couch.*)

COCO: Nell—what about me?

(COCO *watches as* SCOTT *moves on top of* NELL.)

BRENT: Happy. That's a hard one. *(Pause)* It's taking me so long to answer because I'm thinking about it. A lot of people, they say you can't answer all at once, right away, it means you don't know the answer, it isn't a true answer. I don't think that. I never have. *(Pause)* Yeah. It made me happy. *(Pause. Very satisfied)* Yeah.

(BRENT *looks over, sees* NELL *and* SCOTT. NELL *is still not responding to* SCOTT's *caresses, but she's not resisting either.*)

BRENT: Hey, man, what are you doing? Hey buddy. Buddy?

SCOTT: Drinking. I'm drunk. Driving. I hope to never see a car again as long as I live. Womanizing...well, you're a woman. This is as close as it gets.

BRENT: Hey, man. What about me? What about me?

SCOTT: What about you?

BRENT: She don't want you, she wants me.

COCO: That's right. You tell him. *(She rushes over to* BRENT, *tries to get him to stand up.)* You stop them!

BRENT: Let's talk this out, man to man, ole buddy—

SCOTT: Shut up. Can't you see I'm busy?

(BRENT *sags back onto the floor.*)

COCO: Nell, please—we had a deal!

BRENT: *(Weakly)* Buddy, you're making a terrible mistake.

COCO: *(To* BRENT) Then do something! Do something!

BRENT: I don't feel so good.

COCO: Nell. I'm begging you—Nell? *(No response. She kneels next to BRENT and holds him to her.)* Nell? Oh, Nell.

(COCO kisses BRENT. NELL immediately pushes SCOTT away from her, roughly, and gets up from the couch. She pulls COCO away from BRENT. SCOTT jumps up.)

SCOTT: What are you doing to me, honey? Ole Brent didn't tell me you were a tease. I didn't come here, bargaining on a tease.

(NELL pushes COCO over to SCOTT, who catches her in his arms. He hesitates, then pushes her back.)

SCOTT: Hey! What kind of game are we playing here? Musical lips? I'm not interested in playing musical lips!

NELL: *(Pushing COCO into SCOTT's arms again)* You won't know the difference.

SCOTT: The hell I won't!

NELL: For a minute. For two. But what's a minute or two? In a minute or two—where you'll be—well, you know where you want to be.
    When you know where you want to be—it's all the same.

SCOTT: What are you talking about?

NELL: You're getting married in the morning.

COCO: *(Frightened)* Give me a minute—just a—

NELL: Now.

(NELL pushes COCO closer to SCOTT. COCO kisses him.)

SCOTT: Well. Little Carol Crandal. Well. Well. Well.

(SCOTT kisses COCO, and starts to unbutton her blouse. He strokes her with his bad hand. She starts to respond, then pulls away.)

SCOTT: Can't stand the heat, get out of the kitchen.

(COCO *hesitates, then takes* SCOTT *over to the couch. She turns to* NELL *for help.*)

COCO: Nell—

NELL: I'm here.

COCO: I'm frightened.

NELL: (*She kneels down in front of them, takes* COCO's *hand and puts it over* SCOTT's *heart.*) The center of the earth, Coco, think how hot it is there. Think how you can get there. Think how it blots out the entire world. How when you get there there's nothing behind you and nowhere else to go.

(COCO *takes* SCOTT's *face in her hands and kisses his eyes, his mouth, his chest.*)

NELL: How it burns you clean, and binds you up. And the fire ball's all—

COCO/NELL: —around you. Holding you up. Pressing into you.

NELL: And there is that one moment—

COCO/NELL: And there is that moment when you stop caring about anything.

COCO: But this. When none of it but this makes any sense. When you realize, none of it ever did. When you know that if the world is ever to be destroyed, it will happen now. It has happened already. You know it has been. The fall, the fire, the bomb has been dropped. And it has all passed away.

(COCO *and* SCOTT *sink back on the couch.*)

COCO: I love you.

NELL: (*Turns to* BRENT) I love you.

SCOTT: (*Releases* COCO *abruptly*) What the hell are you talking about?

COCO: I love you. I've loved you ever since I saw you fall—

SCOTT: *(Standing up)* What is this center of the earth crap, anyway? You're talking figuratively, huh? How do you figure you can talk figuratively about the center of the earth? It's there. It's a mass of molten rock. It's a place where stone runs like slow water.

How do you figure you can talk figuratively about the center of the earth? Once upon a time, before we knew what it was like down there, maybe then it was a very romantic place. But you get to the center of the earth nowadays, you know what you get? Steamrolled. You get spread out thin enough to wrap around the panhandle of Oklahoma. *(Furious)* Now you tell me. Who the hell wants to get wrapped around the panhandle of Oklahoma?

NELL: *(To* BRENT*)* I love you.

SCOTT: I mean, it sounds very nice, but it doesn't change it. What the hell you gonna do in the center of the earth? *(Pause)* I'll tell you. *(He grabs* COCO *by the shoulders.)* YOU CAN'T DO NOTHING IN THE CENTER OF THE EARTH!

NELL: I love you.

BRENT: *(Lifts his head up—obviously a tremendous effort to speak)* No.

SCOTT: *(Goes over to* BRENT. *Shakes him)* Ole buddy, we got to get moving. I'm getting married. In the morning.

COCO: *(Screaming at* NELL*)* Why didn't you tell me it was just a story!

SCOTT: Come on, man, we got to go!

COCO: *(Sobbing)* It isn't there, it isn't there! *(She hides her face in her arms.)* I want to go home. I want to go home. I want— *(Softly)* Steven. Oh my God, Steven— *(She stands up, moves uncertainly toward the phone.)*

SCOTT: Come on, man, we got to go. Now—

NELL: Brent—I didn't mean it—tell me you don't believe me! Tell me I never told you—

(SCOTT *drags* BRENT *toward the door as* COCO *dials the phone.)*

BRENT: I gotta go.

COCO: Steven! Oh, Steven— *(She sobs into the phone, uncontrollably.)*

NELL: *(To* BRENT *as he is carried through the door)* I love you—

COCO: No, no, I want you to come right now—I don't care, come now...get me out of here, now...no, she's not—SHE'S NOT!—because I SAY SHE'S NOT—please, Steven, hurry...please hurry.

NELL: *(Standing at the window, watching them leave)* I love you.

(Lights fade to blackout)

END OF ACT TWO

ACT THREE

(It is near sunrise.)

(COCO has fallen asleep, cradling the phone in her arms.)

(NELL is standing at the door, holding the screen door shut as BRENT tries to open it.)

NELL: NO!

BRENT: Hey, what's it gonna hurt? *(He struggles to open the door.)* After all, you know what Shakespeare said.

NELL: NO!

BRENT: Sure you do. He said—I think it was him—he said it's sad to those who feel and funny to those who think. *(Pause)* Life is. *(Pause)* Hey, come on, what's it gonna hurt? *(He pulls the door open.)*

NELL: *(Blocking his path)* My sister's sleeping.

BRENT: Well, then, it's sad or funny to her depending on her definition of sleep.

(BRENT tries to get past NELL into the house. She steps outside and closes the door behind her.)

NELL: Come on. It's too...hot inside.

(BRENT and NELL walk around to the side porch, in front of the window.)

BRENT: You're the one who told me that.

NELL: I am?

BRENT: And I said it didn't make any sense, because I spent all my time thinking about how sad it was.

NELL: That's not thinking.

BRENT: Sure it is.

NELL: That's feeling.

BRENT: No, that's thinking. You can think about feeling sad, you know.

NELL: That's not the point.

BRENT: You said you loved me.

NELL: And you said—

BRENT: Yeah. I know what I said.

NELL: You think it's sad.

BRENT: I do not.

NELL: I think it's funny.

BRENT: You can't think about something like that.

NELL: I can't think about anything else.

BRENT: You can't think about it.

NELL: I can.

BRENT: You can think about how it feels.

NELL: It feels funny. Which means I'm thinking about it.

BRENT: I don't think you can tell the difference.

NELL: I can. That's the trick. Can't teach an old dog new tricks—well I say you can. It's the only trick I ever learned and I'm going to stick with it.

BRENT: Here's a joke Scott told me after we left. "Daycart said" —I'm saying that right, aren't I? "Daycart said: To do is to be. Kant said: To be is to do. Sinatra said:

BRENT/NELL: Do-be do-be do."

BRENT: You know it.

NELL: Who doesn't.

BRENT: I didn't.

NELL: It's an old joke.

BRENT: Scott had to tell me who Daycart and Kant were. He told me all about them.

NELL: You don't have to know to get the joke.

BRENT: Like hell you don't. Otherwise, you don't get the joke. Here's these two assholes, spending all their time thinking about what and how and why people feel—wasting their lives writing books full of bullshit—Scott said it was hard-to read-bullshit, too—pissing it all away about doing and being and being and doing and Sinatra—who's got an okay voice but he's a jerk, right, he's a drunk and everybody knows about him and the Mafia, right—Sinatra, who's a jerk, just comes along and he just cuts right through it.

Do-be do-be do.

You gotta love the man for that.

And those two assholes—picture the hemorrhoids those two assholes have got from sitting at a desk all day trying to figure the difference it would make if they could prove the difference.

Do-be, do-be, do. You gotta love ole Frank for that.

NELL: You don't get the joke.

BRENT: The joke's on them. There's no difference! There isn't anything else you can do but do—you can not do, but that's just another kind of doing—and you can be or not, but that's an easy one too. The joke's on them.

NELL: It's a good joke, but it isn't the same joke.

BRENT: Oh, come on, will ya? You just didn't get it before, why won't you admit it? You may have heard it before, but maybe you didn't get it before.

NELL: It's a better joke.

BRENT: Damn right. It's a damn good joke. *(Pause)* You don't think I'm real bright, do you?

NELL: Sometimes I do.

BRENT: Yeah?

NELL: But I know you're not.

BRENT: I was smart enough to get the joke, wasn't I?

NELL: That's what confuses me

BRENT: That dumb Brent got the joke? Well, I got news for you—

NELL: That's what confuses me.

BRENT: What?

NELL: I said, it confuses me. Goddamnit, it confuses me. How can I tell what it is when it confuses me? *(Pause)* Sorry. I'm sorry.

BRENT: S'okay. *(Shrugs)* I know what you think of me. You think I'm a horny guy and a good lay.

NELL: I do not.

BRENT: Not what you feel. What you think. It is what you think, isn't it?

NELL: That isn't the way I think about you.

BRENT: Jesus Christ—

NELL: I think about you all the time and I never think that you're a horny guy and a good lay.

BRENT: Well. *(Pause)* I am.

NELL: Well. Yes. You are.

BRENT: See? That is the way you think about me.

NELL: I do not—

BRENT: OH JESUS CHRIST!

(BRENT's *yelling wakes* COCO *up. She is groggy, disoriented.*)

BRENT: Look. I'm a horny guy and a good lay and you love you. You figure it out.

NELL: No.

BRENT: Okay, don't.

NELL: I think about you all the time.

BRENT: Well I don't know what you're thinking, then. I don't know who you're thinking about.

NELL: You.

BRENT: You spend all your time thinking about a dumb, horny guy you don't think is dumb and horny.

NELL: I don't think about you that way, I—

BRENT: I'm serious. This is making me crazy. We got to stop this. I mean, it just can't keep going on and on in circles like this. It's got to go somewhere. *(Pause)* No. That's not what I meant.

NELL: That's where it goes.

BRENT: Where it went.

(COCO *moves quietly to the window, and hides there, listening.*)

NELL: One year of my life. To the day.

BRENT: One year and a day. That's the funny thing about weeks and years and things. A week is from Monday to Sunday. That's seven days. Monday to Monday is eight. People say a year ago today. They don't mean that. I mean, you think about it.

You can only count one day once. Like with anniversaries, for instance. People are way off. They're counting the day twice. This is the way it should work: You get married, say, on the 31st of June. Your first anniversary should be celebrated on the 30th, see?

And your second on the 29th, third on the 28th and so on. Birthdays should work that way too. By the time a person was forty, they could be three different signs of the Zodiac, if they were lucky. That would really be something, wouldn't it? There are way too many people staying Leos all their lives, if you know what I mean.

And think about the Fourth of July. Think about it. We'd celebrate it in January this year.

NELL: There's no 31st in June.

BRENT: What?

NELL: Thirty days hath September, April, June—

BRENT/NELL: —and November.

BRENT: So.

NELL: So you can't get married on the 31st.

BRENT: We all make mistakes. *(Pause)* That's the beauty of my system. Say you did get married on the 31st—say you make a mistake on the invitations or something—at least you wouldn't have to live with it. You'd never have to make that mistake again. You'd have to live to be four hundred, if you see what I'm saying.

You know what Scott said? Scott said "You can't step in the same river twice." That's what he said as we were driving out of here. I said, who would want to.

He said all kinds of people did but that they couldn't. I said what's the big deal. I said run like a son of a bitch downstream, you'll make it.

I'm trying to talk to you. *(No response)* I sure didn't think it would be this hard, not being in there, doing... you know.

I thought it would be nice just to talk.

NELL: Do you remember it?

BRENT: What?

NELL: A year and a day ago?

BRENT: You mean, in there?

NELL: Yes.

BRENT: That's a lot of running.

NELL: A year and one day. One day. All I'm asking you to remember is one day.

BRENT: Two weeks is about my limit. I'm not, as you pointed out, an especially quick guy.

NELL: One day.

BRENT: Yeah. I remember it. So?

NELL: I just wondered.

BRENT: Who you kidding, lady? Who? "I just wondered." What a joke.

NELL: I did. I wondered.

BRENT: "Wondered."

NELL: For a year.

BRENT: I think I know what you're leading up to. I think I know what you think wondering means. *(Pause)* You don't want to hear me say it, but you asked for it. Because it wasn't. Wonderful. *(Pause)* No matter how fast you figure you been running.

NELL: I know.

BRENT: You sure didn't act like you did.

NELL: I know now, all right? I know it wasn't— *(Whispers)* —wonderful.

BRENT: I don't think so.

NELL: Okay then, don't. *(Sighs, about to get really upset. She has trouble breathing.)* Look—could you go now, please? You told me it wasn't—could you go now? Please?

BRENT: No. See, I'm not done yet. There's something else I've got to say.

  See, I thought it would be a nice thing, if you heard me say I didn't love you.

NELL: Please, go.

BRENT: I thought it might change things.

NELL: And just what did you think you could change?

BRENT: Come on—

NELL: No. Tell me. Just what made you think there's something in me you could change?

BRENT: *(Grabs her, shakes her)* There's guys, drivers on the road, talking about you. Word spreads on the road, that's the way it is, it spreads. There's guys, at truck stops and bars, talking about you.

NELL: So?

BRENT: So I don't like them talking about you. See, I know it's different from what they're saying. I know you're different.

  I knew you were different from the start. What I didn't know was that you were in love. Then, when I knew you were in love, I didn't know, for a long time, that it was with me.

  I don't like you're being in love with me.

NELL: I'm dreaming this.

BRENT: No! That's the point. This is what you're not dreaming. This is what it's not up to you to dream.

NELL: *(Breaking away from him)* Why the hell did you come back? Why!

BRENT: I told you why.

NELL: You were gone! Gone. The door closed behind you. Gone. I heard your car drive away. I could have screamed I love you for an hour, a day, a year—it

wouldn't have brought you back. I DIDN'T WANT
YOU COMING BACK! *(She starts to cry.)* This isn't
right! It isn't fair! I don't know what you're doing here!

BRENT: You know what today is?

NELL: No.

BRENT: Today is the day that will be the 364th
anniversary of the day you met me, 365 years from a
year ago and a day. That's how long it will take for it to
come around again. That's how long it will be if you're
planning on jumping in the same river twice. And
that's not even counting for leap years.

    You're different. I can tell that. That's why those
guys, they made me mad. They were talking about you
but I didn't know it was you they were talking about.
They said "Hey, Brent, we know about where there's
this woman, she's so hot for it, she'll fuck anything.
She'd even fuck a snake. You want her number,
Brent?"

    I didn't have to hit too many of them too hard. I
didn't have to, you see, it's not the kind of thing a guy
has to punch out a lot of guys about. It's just not that
kind of thing.

    But then I found out it was you they were talking
about. What could I do? I would of had to kill 'em all.
It *is* that kind of thing.

    I don't mean to make it worse. I came back to make it
better.

NELL: Your secret is safe.

BRENT: What secret?

NELL: That you wrote down the number of a woman
who'd fuck a snake.

BRENT: Hey, I don't deserve that.

NELL: Okay, so you don't. So just what is it you think
you deserve? Just what is it you want?

BRENT: You're packing up to leave with your sister, aren't you?

NELL: No.

BRENT: Hey, you don't have to hide it from me. I'm the last person you'd have to hide it from. I think it's a great idea. Where you going?

NELL: I'm not going anywhere.

BRENT: I'll bet your sister's from up north. You can always tell the ones from up north from the way they sweat. And your sister was sweating just that way. You know the way I mean. The way they sweat like the heat's some sort of personal insult, like God went to the trouble of heating up three thousand square miles of open country just for the pleasure of watching them sweat.

You think you're gonna like it up there?

NELL: I'm not going up north.

BRENT: I myself have never liked it.

NELL: I hate it. I have been cold once or twice in my life.

BRENT: You're moving up north cause of me, aren't you?

NELL: In a few hours all this will be gone. In a few hours it will all be like a bad dream.

And that was the last thing I wanted. For it to be a bad dream.

BRENT: Look at me. *(Pause)* I don't love you. *(He grabs her arm to hold her there.)* One more thing. And then I'll go.

I'm of two minds of how to do this. All the way back from dropping Scottie off I thought, now how's the best way to do this.

I thought that maybe if I came back and said I loved

you, that that might do it. But that would only work if
you didn't really love me. See, I've heard that there's
lots of women like that—they love you and love you
and love you, and the minute you break down and say
you love them, they stop loving you.

It's a shame, isn't it? That there isn't a little more logic
to it all. But there's no two ways about it.

Even if you didn't really love me, I still wouldn't love
you.

So there I was, stuck, you see, stuck on how was
the best way to do it. There I was, tearing on across
the desert, keeping her steady, at first, at ninety, then
ninety-five, then pushing her up over the top and
nursing her there, holding her just under what I knew
she could do, what you think, sometimes, alone on the
desert, she almost tells you she wants you to do...

And then I remembered something my father said.

My father said: Always leave 'em wanting more.

NELL: Is this your idea of a joke? You really think
there's anything you could do that would make me
want you more? I've wanted you every night with
every man I could find who made me want you. I can't
want you any more.

BRENT: That's what you think you were doing? You
think you were doing it for me?

NELL: What else have I done but want you? And want
you more and more?

BRENT: Wanting? And wanting? And wanting?

NELL: Yes.

BRENT: Nope. Getting. And getting. That's what you
were doing.

NELL: That sounds like something your friends at the
truck stop would say.

BRENT: I didn't say they were my friends. Although there's quite a number of 'em claim to be yours.

NELL: You don't like what they're saying? They're saying it because of you. Doesn't that mean anything?

BRENT: Only that you're getting more and enjoying it less.

NELL: You goddamn stupid son of a—

BRENT: HEY! You're talking about the man you love!

NELL: What do you want from me? JUST WHAT THE HELL DO YOU WANT!

BRENT: What I want from you is for it to have to do with me.

NELL: What are you talking about—

BRENT: Me, that's what I'm talking about.

NELL: But—

BRENT: I'm talking about me. I'm talking about what I want. I'm talking about giving you something you can't get just by wanting it.

NELL: You're crazy—

BRENT: I want to leave you wanting something it's not so simple for you to just answer the phone, and get.

NELL: No—*I'm* crazy. No—dreaming. I was dreaming.

BRENT: That's some bad, bad dream. I'd hate to wake up after a year like that.

I'd hate to have to say I could sleep through three hundred and sixty-six nights spent with as many men doing what men like to do as you're going to have to tell yourself you slept through.

Always leave 'em wanting more. That's what my father told me. Leave 'em wanting more. Do you think that's a good thing or a bad thing? (*No response*) I'm going to kiss you, and then I'm going to go.

(NELL *backs away from* BRENT.)

NELL: No. I don't want you to.

BRENT: You've kissed me before.

NELL: What if it costs me another year? It's stopped now, I want it to stay stopped.

BRENT: You don't know what you want. I'm the living, breathing proof of that one.

(BRENT *tries to pull* NELL *to him.*)

NELL: Please—don't. Don't make me remember—look what you did when you kissed me.

BRENT: I never really kissed you.

(BRENT *pulls* NELL *close.*)

NELL: I'll wake up tomorrow morning, and I won't remember this. It will just be another part of the dream, the part that's gone away.

BRENT: I didn't back track two hundred miles over the ugliest part of America in the dead of night to have you forget me.

See, it's like this. Leaving 'em wanting more is a good thing, if what you gave 'em was so good they just naturally want more of it. But maybe they want more because, good as it was, it wasn't enough. Or maybe it wasn't good enough. Or maybe—

Maybe it wasn't good at all.

Maybe what you gave 'em was something bad.

Maybe what you gave 'em was something bad, and what you left 'em was wanting more.

You see my point? (*He kisses her gently.*)

And I want to see you smile.

(NELL *hesitates, then can't help smiling.*)

BRENT: I'm gone. (*He turns, walks down the front steps, and is gone.*)

(The sound of his car starting up, driving away)

(NELL stands for a few moments, watching him leave in the by now bright sunrise. She goes inside. COCO, standing by the door, grabs her arm.)

COCO: Nell—

NELL: What— *(Breaking away)*

COCO: Wait a minute, Nell—I want to tell you something.

(NELL ignores COCO.)

COCO: Nell I'm talking to you!

NELL: *(Turns to face her)* Why? You gonna say you're sorry, Coco? There's nothing for you to be sorry about.

COCO: I'm not sorry.

NELL: *(Shrugs)* Good. *(Strongly)* Because neither am I. Not sorry at all.

COCO: *(Softly)* I know.

NELL: *(Superior)* No, I don't think so.

COCO: Fact?

NELL: Don't, Coco.

COCO: Fact? Come on, Nell, *FACT?*

NELL: What if I say it? If I say fact, what do you say? What comes next?

COCO: I say—liar. I say—confess.

NELL: And then, when I won't confess?

COCO: I say—I love you.

NELL: And after that?

COCO: After that there's nothing left.

(NELL holds COCO.)

COCO/NELL: *(So softly, it is barely heard)* I love you.

(NELL *holds* COCO.)

COCO/NELL: *(So softly, it is barely heard)* I love you.

COCO: What was kissing him like?

NELL: Just now? Oh, not much. Kinda—well, sweet.

COCO: Not like it was before.

NELL: Oh…no.

COCO: Not the kind of thing you'd chase after for a year, I guess.

NELL: No. Not at all.

COCO: Does that make you sad?

NELL: *(Pause)* At a certain point, you know you'll have to come home. Even if you're on a rocket ship of a kiss, even if you've made it all the way to—Jupiter, Saturn, the stars, even if you've turned the entire universe into him—at a certain point, it's like King Midas, you know? You want to eat a meal or take a walk or see another man who doesn't make you think of him. You want to come home. Not because you're tired. Just because—you've gotten as far as you can go. I'm glad he came back. It's time I came home.

COCO: You're so brave. I could never be brave like you.

NELL: You don't mean that. You think I'm tragic.

COCO: No, I don't.

NELL: You're lying to me, and you're—

COCO: If they gave a medal for this, you'd get one.

NELL: For what—seeing something that's not there? For trying to see it everywhere anyway?

COCO: For falling in love. Fairy tales are full of love at first sight, aren't they? And nobody thinks they're tragic.

NELL: Right, because in fairytales, when you fall in love, someone falls back. You both fall.

COCO: That just proves how much harder this is, how much more you deserve a medal.

NELL: Yeah, well, I don't think anyone's going to give me one for unrequited love.

COCO: Well they should. You'd call me, and tell me what it was like and I wanted to tell the whole world how brave you were. But I knew I couldn't. I knew no one would understand. Oh, if you'd been my brother, I could have told everybody. And the men would have been jealous, and called you a lucky son of a bitch, and the women would have been dreamy and sad no one ever loved them that much in an instant like that. But you weren't my brother, you were my sister.

One night I tried to tell Steven—

NELL: Oh no, that would be a huge mistake—

COCO: I know, I don't know what came over me. I started—then I came to my senses. I was dying to tell him, but I couldn't. So I told the kids.

NELL: What?

(COCO sits on the couch, has NELL lie with her head in her lap.)

COCO: You were turning the whole world into him— you were performing a high wire death defying magic act. I had to tell someone, didn't I? So I told the kids a bedtime story. But you know how I am with stories. So I told them—you're going to laugh—I told them the one about the Princess and the Pea.

NELL: They're too old for the Princess and the Pea.

COCO: Yes. They are. But I told it anyway. And when I was through, you know what Jeffery said? He said there was something wrong with that Princess. There was obviously something wrong with a person who could feel something no one else in the world could feel. And there was something crazy about the people who went and gave her a kingdom because of it.

NELL: Oh, wow.

COCO: Yeah. Ten years old and he's got the sensitivity of a thirty-five year old beer drinking lout. I don't know what I'm going to do about that. But Melissa got it. She understood.

NELL: I don't know if that's good or not. *(She sits up.)*

COCO: Of course it's good. You're not sorry it happened. If you had to do it over again—

NELL: It's the kind of thing you only need to do once in a lifetime, I think. I've done it. Once was enough for me.

COCO: Oh, come home with me, Nell. It's August, but it's cool. In the evenings. In the shade. Come home with me.

NELL: What will Steven say?

COCO: About what?

NELL: About me.

COCO: That you got the wrong stuff under your bed.

NELL: *(Laughing)* No. I meant about when you called him last night.

COCO: I'll just tell him we a bad dream, and woke up, afraid.

NELL: All right. I'll go. And in a week or two, I'll come back home. I'm ready to come back now.

Coco: Then come on, let's get you packed—

(NELL lies back down with her head in COCO's lap before COCO can get up.)

NELL: No. Let's stay here.

COCO: But Steven'll be here any minute—

NELL: Yes. Any minute. So until he gets here, let's just stay like this.

(Slow fade to blackout)

END OF PLAY

9 780881 454475